Winston Churchill

A Biography of a British Prime Minister

Joseph Greene

Table of Contents

Introduction 1

Chapter 1: Churchill's Early Days 3

Chapter 2: From War to Peace and Politics 13

Chapter 3: The First World War 24

Chapter 4: After the War.. 34

Chapter 5: The Prophecy Comes True 40

Chapter 6: Waging the Second World War 45

Conclusion... 51

References 54

Introduction

Sir Winston Leonard Spencer Churchill's seemingly evergreen legacy has lived long past his death on January 24, 1965. He was a man who, despite the challenges he faced over the course of his life, showed great determination, intellect, political wisdom, and unparalleled leadership skills.

Churchill was born on November 30, 1874, into a world much different than our own, yet there is much we can and should learn from his story. Men and women whose legacies persist long after their deaths are worth taking note of, either for their exemplary good and accomplishments or their despicable evils. We learn either way. As Churchill himself said, "Those that fail to learn from history are doomed to repeat it".

Churchill remains one of the most famous British prime ministers, and he was, among other things, also a father, husband, statesman, orator, and author of books such as *This Was Their Finest Hour, Victory,* and *The End of The Beginning.*

The story begins with Churchill's low beginnings in poverty and culminates at the heights that allowed him to rally the British people and take them from teetering on the edge of defeat in World War II to historically renowned victory.

He rose to political prominence before World War I, and over the course of his political career, he came into conflict or alliance with some of history's other big names, like Adolf Hitler, Joseph Stalin, and Franklin D. Roosevelt, among others. Moreover, Churchill played a key role in defeating Hitler, halting the expansion of the Soviet Union, and leading the conservatives back into office in 1951.

Considering and learning from these accomplishments allows us to consider our own present moment and understand how we can correct our course moving forward.

Chapter 1: Churchill's Early Days

Born November 30, 1874, in Blenheim Palace, Oxfordshire, England, Churchill grew up with little familial love or academic prosperity.

His parents married in April 1874, but their prestigious backgrounds did little to compensate for their lack of availability in Churchill's life. Churchill's father, Lord Randolph Henry Spencer-Churchill, was a Conservative politician, and his mother, Jennie Jerome, was the daughter of a New York stockbroker.

While growing up and learning the ways of his world and people, young Winston Churchill was taken care of by his caring nanny, Mrs. Everest. He and his younger brother, Jack (born February 4, 1880) spent their early lives at boarding schools in Ascot and Brighton before Winston was sent to Harrow School.

Churchill started at St. Georges School near Ascot, Berkshire on November 3, 1882, and two years later, in 1884, entered Misses Thompson's School. On April 17, 1888, Churchill entered Harrow School, which was founded in 1572 by John Lyon under a Royal Charter of Queen Elizabeth I.

The boys lived through what we now consider major historical landmarks, including Alexander Graham Bell's first telephone call, made on March 10, 1876, Edison's invention of the phonograph in 1877, the earliest known football match involving Manchester United in 1882, the publishing of the first part of the 1st edition of the Oxford English Dictionary on February 1, 1884, the fountain pen patent received by L E Waterman in 1884, and the first Coca-Cola sale in 1886.

Churchill's school days were all but enjoyable, a common theme among great minds of the past. Through all his intellectual and academic failures at Harrow, there were some signs of brilliance that he let shine forth now and then. For example, Churchill won a competition at Harrow for reciting 1,200 lines of Macaulay's long poem *Lays of Ancient Rome* from memory alone and won the 1892 Public Schools Fencing Championship.

However, these feats did little to shrink the growing pile of failures accumulated during his time at Harrow. Churchill himself wrote that "I was on the whole considerably discouraged by my school days". Despite these failures and challenges, there was something different within Churchill. Similar to other brilliant leaders such as Alexander the Great, Churchill felt a greater destiny calling him from a young age. Even as a boy, he would gaze up at the tapestries covering the walls of Blenheim Palace while visiting his grandparents, the Duke and Duchess of Marlborough.

The tapestries were a sight to behold for any man or woman who was fortunate enough to see them—their colors, stories, and the faces within those mounted frames would be enough to catch anyone's eye. But for Churchill, they were more than just impressive paintings. They were testaments to his bloodline's greatness that foreshadowed his own legacy. Those tapestries depicted the battles and victories of John Churchill, 1st Duke of Marlborough. A man who was remembered for his time on the battlefield, his bloodline led all the way down to young Winston Churchill, who stared up at those depictions of his ancestor's victories with a growing sense of purpose.

So convinced was he of his success, that while in Harrow suffering from his failures, he told a friend that "I shall be in command of the defenses of London... In the high position I shall occupy, it will fall to me to save the Capital and save the Empire". And that he did.

Into The 4th Hussars

Due to his obvious interest in the military and poor academic performance at Harrow, Churchill's father decided to enter him into the army. Even as a child, Churchill displayed many qualities befitting a soldier, such as his strong willpower and determination. In the eyes of others, his rebelliousness and seeming lack of intellect seemed to hold him back. He seemed far too impotent to even worm his way into a university, and this view that others had of him was only further enforced when he failed the entrance exam to the Royal Military College twice before passing on his third attempt. Perhaps the mere fact that he took it a third time was demonstrative of his determined nature.

This enrollment shattered the wall that stood in his way of success. In 1894, he graduated 20th in his class of 130. This small victory was a ramp that, in 1895, led to him entering the 4th Hussars, also known as the Queen's Own 4th Hussar. The 4th Hussars was a cavalry regiment in the British Army that was first formed in 1685, with battle honors that included the Peninsular War against Napoleon in 1808-14, the First Afghan War of 1839-42, and the Crimean War of 1854-55.

In 1895, he received his first commission from the Queen, which was effective on February 20th. The money paid to a newly minted second Lieutenant was only £120 a year, a relatively small sum. But his newfound success—and possibly the desire to prove himself after his father's death—seemed to spur him on in his efforts and goals for the future.

A year in the regimental life of an officer permitted five months of extended periods of leave, leaving the other seven months for training, which mostly consisted of drills and provided ample time to play polo.

Aware of the fact that his regiment would be sent to India the following year, and unwilling to let his hand rest in the presence of opportunity, Churchill took up tasks of his own during the five months of leave, while others in the Hussars took time off and enjoyed the pleasures that money could buy. Unlike them, Churchill had little money but much to prove.

He first went to Cuba and spent several months reporting on the Cuban war of independence from Spain for the London Daily Graphic. This was more of an adventure-seeking move than a career-oriented one, but it was nonetheless a powerful step that forced him to prove his courage to himself. As he himself wrote about choosing to go to Cuba: "I thought it might be as well to have a private rehearsal, a secluded trial trip in order to make sure that the ordeal was not unsuited to my temperament".

In 1895, Cuba was still a Spanish colony. Spain's attempts at halting the rebellion included 200,000 troops, among whom Churchill and his traveling companion, Lieutenant Reggie Barnes, soon joined. The two lieutenants arrived in Havana on November 20th, and on the 28th, joined a fighting column under Spanish General Valdez as observers. They stayed with the column for eight days. The war had a lot to offer Churchill. It was the first time he had drawn so near to death and war in its purest form, and he finally had the chance to show himself and everyone else what he was capable of in the face of danger and death. Churchill later wrote:

The 30th of November was my 21st birthday, and on that day for the first time I heard shots fired in anger and heard bullets strike flesh or whistle through the air.

The column traded blows and gunfire with the rebels on and off for around three days, after which Churchill and Barnes left Cuba. Before leaving, in the first week of December 1985, Barnes and Churchill were recommended for the Cross of the Order of Military Merit. Later, in 1914, Churchill received the Cuban Campaign Medal. For sixteen total days spent in Cuba, Churchill had earned two commendations.

Churchill's next adventure began on October 2, 1896, when his regiment went to India by ship. They—Lieutenant Churchill, twenty-two officers, two warrant officers, 448 NCOs, and men—took a train to their station in Bengaluru (Bangalore). This would be Churchill's permanent station until 1899. While his time there proved to be productive by nearly any metric, he said that Bangalore was nothing more to him than a "garrison town which resembles a third-rate watering hole," and described his life in such conditions as "stupid, dull and uninteresting."

But once again, standing still was not an option for him, and true to his character, he quickly found something to entertain himself with. In September 1897, Churchill joined the Malakand Field Force on the Northwest Frontier of India and served as both a reporter and a soldier some 2,000 miles from Bangalore. He started as a correspondent but quickly climbed the ranks to join the commanding general's staff. He wrote to his family during this time, saying:

> I am bound for many reasons to risk something... I mean to play this game out and if I lose, it is obvious that I could never have won any other... I am more ambitious for a reputation for personal courage than anything else in the world. A young man should worship a young man's ideals.

Similarly to Cuba, India had its own experiences to share with young Churchill. On September 16, 1897, Churchill was with the Field Force in Mahmoud Valley when, while covering a company withdrawal from a village in the area, the company came under attack. Churchill had to withstand and survive gunfire that poured on for 13 hours, all the while keeping his wits and helping other soldiers where he could. For instance, he assisted another soldier in carrying a wounded ally to safety while being shot at. This was a demonstration of true courage, one that in the past had been rewarded with the Victoria Cross, as Lieutenant Lord Fincastle had been a month prior. Churchill himself said that the action "might perhaps, had there been any gallery, have received some notice." Where did this bravery stem from? Similar to those tapestries he used to look up at with sheer determination, the battlefield itself seemed to enhance both his will to survive and his instinct for greatness. "Bullets are not worth considering, Churchill wrote, "I do not believe the Gods would create so potent a being as myself for so prosaic an ending."

That was not the end of the action for Churchill. Later that same month at Agra, he and his regiment once again faced enemy fire. This time, the fighting lasted for five unrelenting hours. He believed this conflict in the Northwest Frontier to be one of the worst in forty years. It was no easy country to fight in. For one, the temperature disparity between England and India would have been debilitating.

In this battle at Agra, fifty were left seriously wounded, many of the soldiers were branded for life with scars, and seventeen took their last breath on that soil. Among the dead was the regimental commander. Even amidst the bloodshed and chaos, Churchill prevailed as the brave-hearted survivor. So impressive was his conduct in the midst of the hazy turmoil of battle that the dispatches of the Malakand Field Force mentioned him directly. They read "Brigadier Jeffries has praised the courage and resolution of Lieutenant W L. S. Churchill 4th Hussars, the correspondent of the Pioneer Newspaper with the Force, who made himself useful at a critical moment."

His courage and cool-headed thinking during the battle were what made him stand out among his peers. To be able to think clearly while being shot at in a foreign country while temperatures soar is no easy feat, even for a seasoned veteran. Churchill's one fear, according to Colonel McVean of the 45th Sikhs, Churchill's tent mate in the Malakand, was getting wounded in the mouth, which would mean he couldn't talk.

Despite his bravery and accomplishments in India, Churchill did not win the much hoped-for Victoria Cross or the Distinguished Service Order, the two highest awards for heroism in the British military. He did, however, receive the India Medal in 1895, clasp Punjab Frontier 1897-98. This medal may seem insignificant when juxtaposed with the others, but there is an important fact to consider: It wasn't just a participation trophy. In order to receive this medal, one had to have been in combat, which Churchill was for about six weeks. The Northwest Frontier was also the birthplace of Churchill's first book, *The Story of the Malakand Field Force*. With these accomplishments under his belt, he moved on to pursue that higher purpose that seemed to be following him around, fueling his tenacity and fearlessness.

Following India, Churchill sought to join an expedition to the Tirah, which never got off the ground; later he aimed to join General Kitchener's campaign to reconquer Sudan from the Dervishes. He enlisted the not inconsiderable help of his mother, writing to her saying:

> Oh, how I wish I could work you up over Egypt! I know you could do it with all your influence—and all the people you know. It is a pushing age and we must shove with the

best. After Tirah and Egypt—then I think I shall turn from war to peace and politics.

Many of those who met Churchill liked and even admired him, and some of his acquaintances were quite influential. But his character and service were not appreciated by all. There were some who criticized Churchill's motives. They called him a medal hunter and glory seeker, their criticisms likely stemming from his seeming need for conflict and self-approval.

Some such criticisms were warranted. He was, after all, trying to reach a higher purpose. He had been trying to make himself known through his battlefield exploits, which he then reported on to the newspapers, an understandably devious-sounding ploy. Some called him "bumptious," meaning irritatingly self-assertive.

In a word, Churchill was overconfident. His invincible attitude was either a magnet or repulsive, depending on who you asked. No doubt some of his critics were simply jealous of his achievements, but those who were genuine critics of his character probably lived with the view that pride is the precursor to a crash. Moreover, the war itself was, for the most part, free of potentially fatal conflicts. Churchill later wrote:

> This kind of war was full of fascinating thrills. It was not like the Great War. No one expected to be killed. The chance of being killed was only a sporting element in a splendid game.

Even so, most young men would've rather stayed home from war, not run headlong into it as Churchill did. Later, his efforts to get into Sudan succeeded, and he was notified by the War Office that he had been attached as a supernumerary Lieutenant to the 21st Lancers for the Sudan campaign with the provision that, in the unlikely event of his death, no additional cost would be placed upon the British Army Funds. Even with such sobering words behind him, he continued doing what he did best.

The 21st Lancers arrived in Cairo on August 2, 1898. Almost two months later, on September 28, they engaged in a charge that was later described as "one of the last several cavalry charges in the history of the British Army." During this 2-minute-long conflict, 310 soldiers engaged with the enemy, and 71 were either killed or wounded. Out of the twenty-eight British soldiers killed in the Battle of Omdurman, twenty-one lost their lives during this conflict. The 21st Lancers were on a reconnaissance mission between the main battle and the City of Khartoum, where they spotted a row of 150 spear men, and charged into a bloody engagement that nearly cost Churchill his life. In the end, there were a few factors that saved him: his position on the battlefield, an old injury, and his weapon.

During this engagement, Churchill was on the far-right side of the battle line, where the fighting was much less intense. It was still an extremely dangerous situation, one that he recalled being "most exhilarating" in conversation with his private secretary and British diplomat, Anthony Montague Browne. Ultimately, his place on the battle line saved his life.

In addition to his fortunate position, an old shoulder injury had rendered Churchill unable to wield a sword, so he was given a Mauser automatic pistol instead, a weapon that proved most useful in ensuring an advantageous distance from the melee.

The Battle of Omdurman was described as:

> a triumph of technology over manpower. This was a new kind of warfare where spearmen faced machine guns. It reminds one of the old British saying, "When all is said we have got the maxim gun and they have not." It was a very violent battle. The British suffered 175 casualties, their

Egyptian allies 307; but the Dervish force had 9,700 killed, between 10,000 and 16,000 wounded and 5,000 taken prisoner.

His time in Sudan earned him the Queen's Sudan Medal and the Khedive's Sudan Medal with clasp for "Khartoum." He also went on to publish *The River War*, a book that is still viewed as one of the greatest historical accounts of the conquest of Sudan between 1896-1899 by Anglo-Egyptian forces led by Lord Kitchener and is often regarded as some of Churchill's most ambitious writing. Churchill's time with the 4th Hussars ended in 1899, as he resigned from the army, effective May 5, 1899. In 1898, after already deciding to leave the army the following year, Churchill played in the all-India polo tournament as part of the 4th Hussars team. He returned to India in December 1898 to participate; naturally, they won the championship trophy.

So often, men and women who have accomplishments and medals behind their inflated egos are as empty as balloons and will pop as soon as one merely approaches with a needle. Churchill, on the other hand, despite his overconfidence and bumptiousness, was not one to shy away in the face of embarrassment and humor. He may have had an ego, but his ego matched his words. His ego wasn't fragile, and this lack of fragility consistently proved useful in many areas of his life.

Chapter 2: From War to Peace and Politics

For five years after Sandhurst, Churchill's broadened horizons and self-application allowed him to see the results of his own hard work and brilliance. During that time, he combatted the tedium of army life in India through a study program intended to make up for his poor academic performance at Harrow and Sandhurst. After his resignation from the army in 1899, Churchill decided to enter politics and make a living through his writings.

Back in England, he decided to try standing as a Conservative at Oldham, where he narrowly lost a by-election. While this loss was no doubt disappointing, he didn't let it slow him down. As a recovery session, in October 1899, he went to South Africa, which is also when the Second Anglo-Boer War erupted. Churchill traveled to South Africa as a correspondent for the Morning Post in London and arrived in Cape Town on October 31, 1899. Britain's aim in this war was to "enforce its interests and the rights and claims of British immigrants in the independent Boer Republics of Natal and Cape Colony."

Two weeks after his arrival, Captain Aylmer Haldane invited him to accompany troops on an armored train reconnaissance near Ladysmith at Estcourt. During the scouting, the train was attacked and derailed by Boer rebels. As usual, Churchill reacted with calm courage. While under fire, he reportedly rallied the soldiers with the cry, "Keep cool, men. This will be interesting for my paper."

He was instrumental in clearing the line, which allowed the locomotive to escape with the wounded. Then, in a stunning show of bravery and comradery, Churchill refused to leave and instead went back for Captain Haldane, which resulted in Churchill's capture. This time, it was his lack of a firearm that saved his life. Had he not left it on the train, the Boer rebels would have found a British soldier with an automatic pistol in hand and a fearless spirit in his eyes and would have likely killed him then and there. Not for the last time, Churchill slipped through the clutches of death. Later accounts by Churchill's contemporaries showed that most thought his bravery was of the highest degree and that he should be awarded a Victoria Cross.

Little did his captors know how much they were helping him by temporarily extinguishing his freedom. He spent his 25th birthday in captivity in Pretoria, the now capital city of South Africa, but after only one month, he escaped.

Typical of Churchill, he ensured that theatrics entered even into his escape from rebel captors. So enthralling were the tales of these theatrics that he gained international notoriety. He climbed over the prison wall, hopped a freight train, hid in a coal mine and, with the help of friendly Englishmen, eventually rode another train to freedom over the border to Portuguese East Africa.

The news of his arrival in Durban on December 23, 1899, was the good news Britain needed during the dark beginning of that war. More importantly, Churchill had accomplished his goal. Though his dreams of being a heroic soldier had fallen short, his heroism as a war correspondent launched him to new heights.

Even with enough fame and stories to last a lifetime, he obtained a commission in the South African Light Horse, an irregular cavalry regiment commanded by Julienne Byng. The following six months took Churchill all over South Africa, even back to the place where he had saved the armored train. During his travels, he participated in many battles across the country, including the battle at Acton Holmes, Potgieter's Drift, Spion Kop, Tugela

River, and the Reliefs of Ladysmith and Pretoria. At Dewetsdorp, Churchill found himself under fire; he was rescued by trooper Clement Roberts, who won the Distinguished Conduct Medal for this feat.

In 1900, Churchill arranged a commission for his younger brother, Jack Churchill, and had him come down to South Africa. His stay was not the most enjoyable, though. Unlike his older brother, who was seemingly invincible to death and severe injury, Jack was shot by a Boer while next to Winston. Churchill reportedly said, "Jack, you silly ass. You've only been here five minutes and you've got yourself shot." Jack, fortunately, recovered after being nursed back to health by his mother, who had come to South Africa as a volunteer on a hospital ship.

Some time after his final battle of the war, General Ian Hamilton wrote, "Winston gave the embattled hosts of Diamond Hill an exhibition of conspicuous gallantry for which he never received full credit." Much to Churchill's great disappointment, he never received a Victoria Cross or a Distinguished Service Order. As he later told Anthony Montague Browne, "I have many medals for adventure, but none for bravery."

This lack of recognition may have stemmed from something other than bad luck. Frank Rhodes, correspondent for *The Times*, informed Churchill that he had gotten into General Kitchener's bad books, quite literally. Churchill's ambitious and headstrong nature was one that put him at odds with the higher-ups he met across the board, and thus his early books had been critical of the high command. This, combined with Kitchener's view that Churchill was using the army as a launchpad for his own ambitions, and that active service assignments "should be reserved for officers whose careers were at stake", may all explain why Churchill was never decorated for his actions in combat.

He did, however, receive the Queen's South Africa Medal with 6 clasps, each seeming to correspond to a month spent in the country after his escape from the Boers. The clasps themselves were, in actual fact, for each battle served: Queen's South Africa Medal 1899-1902 (clasps: Diamond Hill, Johannesburg, Relief of Ladysmith, Orange Free State, Tugela Heights, Cape Colony).

In the end, Churchill's self-perpetuating campaign in South Africa not only made him famous, but also gave him the inspiration and material needed to write another two books: *London to Ladysmith*, featuring the armored train incident, and *Ian Hamilton's March*, based on his newspaper articles.

His success in politics was foreshadowed by his success in the army, and his success in the army was forged with his own two hands. His ventures in the army were a mere stepping-stone in the grand scheme of things, but they were arguably the most pertinent stepping-stone of his life. The political opportunities and movements he saw later in life were largely built upon the fame he accumulated in the army, but they were indulged due to more than Churchill's past. Churchill's luck, determination, and fearlessness, along with his resourcefulness, intellect, and pride in his country, helped him forge his path. In the end, it was Churchill who forged his own reputation by pursuing the right things and never allowing comfort, fear, or complacency to domesticate him into banality.

Conservative to Liberal

With all of his newfound prestige, he once again laid siege to Oldham in the election of 1900. This time, Churchill ironically succeeded in winning by the same margin that he had initially failed by. Now was the time to strike, as he had even more going for him now than he had before. He was now in Parliament, fortified by the £10,000 his writings and lecture tours had earned him and was in the perfect position to forge his path in politics. Oldham (his seat from 1900-06) was an important cotton-spinning center whose electorate favored the Conservative policy of Protectionism, which advocated for higher duties on cheap foreign textiles.

After his election, Churchill's funds were running low. To amend this, a lecture tour of England was proposed; during this tour, Churchill was to give 29 speeches in 30 days. It was a long and arduous task, one that involved repetitive recollection. But the desire for recognition and much-needed money were far too potent to be cast aside in the name of boredom. "But you must remember how much money means to me and how much I need it for political expense and other purposes," Churchill wrote, "and if I can make £3000 by giving a score of lectures on the big towns throughout England on the purely military aspect of the [Boer] war, it is very hard for me to refuse."

He accepted the prospective tour and ended up earning £3700 for those 29 speeches in November 1900. His speeches were both educational and defensive of the war, and they were more well-received than he had anticipated. In one speech, he defended the tactics that the British employed in South Africa, as they were being accused of having elements constituting "atrocious barbarities" that violated the accepted practices of warfare. Churchill stated:

> "The justification of the measures resorted to in order to put an end to guerrilla warfare is that no methods, however stringent, or painful, or severe, can possibly cost

so much misery as the continuance of the anarchy and disorder now prevailing."

It wasn't all good news, though. The hopes he held for the North American tour were dashed, as he expected to make an additional £3000 over 3 months. This was the minimum number; he hoped to make £5000. He wrote to his mother saying that he would "not go to the United States unless guaranteed at least £1000 a month for three months and I should expect a great deal more. Five thousand pounds is not too much for making oneself so cheap."

In the end, his North American tour lasted just over two months, from December 8, 1900, to February 2, 1901, and netted him less than half of his tour of England: £1600. Shortly after this, however, he made his next big mark in his timeline: his maiden speech.

On February 10, 1901, Churchill returned home from his failed tour of North America and gave his maiden speech in the House of Commons. On the roster before him, however, was the soon-to-be prime minister, David Lloyd George (prime minister from 1916-1922), who gave an inflammatory speech that for the first time seemed to make Churchill doubt himself.

After the Liberals were invited to form a government, Henry Campbell-Bannerman took office as Prime Minister in December 1905. With this shift, Churchill became Under-Secretary of State for the Colonies. Much of his time in this position required his full attention to be on South Africa as it recovered after the end of the Boer War.

Lord Elgin held the post of Colonial Secretary with responsibility for directing all colonial affairs worldwide. As Under-Secretary, Churchill was his chief assistant. Since Elgin was in the House of

Lords, Churchill was the nominal chief spokesman on colonial affairs in the House, much to Elgin's anguish.

This Liberal government, as well as Churchill's new-found position as Under-Secretary, led to a change in Churchill's position in Oldham in 1906:

> Churchill's Free Trader stance and consequent defection to the Liberals was based on national rather than local considerations, but as a result the Oldham Conservative Association passed a resolution that he "had forfeited their confidence in him." Following his deselection at Oldham, Churchill was invited to stand for North West Manchester, one of nine of that city's constituencies, with a tiny electorate of just 10,000, of whom almost a third were Jewish. Churchill polled 5,639 votes with a majority of 1,241.

While Churchill has been unjustly labeled as a racist today, he was a product of his time, as most people held these views in 1899. However, throughout his career, he showed his support for freedom for people of all types. Even Nelson Mandela expressed his admiration of Churchill.

Throughout 1904, Colonial Secretary Joseph Chamberlain openly advocated tariffs, placing the Conservative government in a dilemma. Churchill, a convinced free trader, helped to found the Free Food League in order to combat Chamberlain's proposal for Tariff Reform, which would have included an import tax on food. As such, he was disavowed by his constituents and became increasingly alienated from the Conservative party, disagreeing with its attitudes of retribution and super-patriotism in the Boer War, apparent lack of concern about poverty, outmoded thinking about the military, and its growing protectionism toward trade.

This alienation combined with the Conservative Party's irrevocable attachment to a policy of protective tariffs in 1904 led to Churchill joining the Liberals that same year and helped him garner even more attention for the audacious nature of his attacks on Chamberlain and Balfour. A twenty-nine-year-old Churchill entered the Commons chamber on May 31, 1904, bowed to the Speaker, and crossed the floor. He was now among the Liberals. It was a major turning point but was not surprising to anyone who had paid attention during the build-up to his decision.

Hughligans—a group of young Liberal Imperialist politicians—had been Winston's friends. Their sympathies were more aligned with the Liberal Party since they believed in both a strong Britain and social reform. They would become the "New Liberals." The New Liberals believed social reform would neutralize the political appeal of the Labour Party, the political embodiment of organized labor. Churchill had perfect timing. Following the fall of the Conservative Party, the Liberal Party dominated the government, and opened the way for Churchill's move to ministerial office. It also earned him a reputation for opportunism, and he was distrusted by Conservatives for years to follow.

There were two men in particular who were to blame for his more radical side, two colleagues who influenced and pushed him towards radicalism: John Morley, a political legatee of W.E. Gladstone, and David Lloyd George, the fiery Welsh orator. Churchill stepped into his first ministerial post only ten days after his 31st birthday. His victory in Manchester led to his 1906 appointment as Undersecretary of State for the Colonies in the new Liberal government. Since the Secretary of State was a member of the House of Lords, Churchill also represented the Colonial Office in the Commons. This meant that, while he was a Junior Minister, he had an unusually large amount of power at his fingertips. Churchill's knowledge of South Africa, his familiarity with its leaders, and his empathy for the defeated adversary contributed to him being recognized as an able defender of South Africa's policy of conciliation and self-government and the drafting of a new constitution for the Transvaal. This is widely regarded as one of his best early acts of statesmanship.

Churchill became president of the Board of Trade with a seat in the cabinet when the government was reconstructed in 1908 under Prime Minister Herbert H. Asquith. He was defeated in the ensuing Manchester by-election but won at Dundee.

Four years prior, in 1904, Churchill had met a young woman named Clementine Hozier at a party. He was instantly struck by her beauty but didn't get to speak to her. Churchill was a two-edged blade in that he could either be very charming or painfully difficult to deal with. His accomplishments and reputation followed him like a beast that warded away other men who might have challenged him otherwise. In the end, it was his wife who had the strong will and brains to stand up to him, and once they were paired, she stood up for him for the rest of his life.

Four years after their first meeting, he and Clementine spent time together for around a month before getting married in 1908. In the end, it was her beauty and her intellect that appealed to him, as this was a potent combination for a man who was as ambitious as they came. They wrote to one another whenever apart, and sometimes communicated important feelings by letter even when under the same roof.

Theirs was a great romance but, just as importantly, Clementine would dispense wise advice on all of the matters of the day. He relied heavily on her for her unwavering support and for her always-sage advice. Their marriage provided him with a secure and happy backdrop for his turbulent career and proved to be an arrangement of love and affection that helped both through hard times.

Following his marriage, Churchill's appointment to the Board of Trade in 1908 meant that he became a Cabinet member at just 33 years of age. Churchill immediately took the lead in a series of social reforms that would define the New Liberal Party. He became the Party's principal spokesman, sometimes speaking in place of the Prime Minister. Not all of Churchill's initiatives would be achieved during his tenure, but he was instrumental in the movement of liberalism away from laissez-faire and toward social reform at the Board of Trade. During his tenure, he completed the work that Lloyd George had begun on the bill that imposed an eight-hour maximum day for miners. As a result of his efforts, trade boards with the power to fix minimum wages and state-run labor exchanges were established in order to combat the evils of "sweated" labor. The effects of his efforts included limiting mine working hours, labor exchanges, an early type of unemployment office to help men find work, unemployment insurance, a "sweatshops" bill to protect workers from exploitation, a "War against Poverty" to establish old age pensions, and the "Standing Court of Arbitration" to settle labor disputes.

This task was not an easy one. When this Liberal program necessitated high taxation, which in turn provoked the House of Lords to the revolutionary step of rejecting the budget of 1909, Churchill was Lloyd George's closest ally in developing the provocative strategy designed to clip the wings of the upper chamber. Churchill became president of the Budget League, and his oratorical broadsides at the House of Lords were as lively and devastating as Lloyd George's own.

In 1911, the Germans made the inflammatory move of sending a gunboat to Agadir, a port in Morocco, which at the time, was under French control. In light of a Franco-German conflict, Churchill knew that standing with France was to be the best choice.

Lord of the Admiralty

The ministerial post of First Lord of the Admiralty is the civilian head of the British Royal Navy. Churchill was appointed to the coveted post in late 1911 and, like most things that he did, he took it up with great gusto. It was as if he foresaw World War One and instantly set to preparing the navy. The first order of business was the task of creating a naval war staff. While Britain had a lead over Germany's naval forces, the Germans were slowly growing in power. So, in typical Winston style, he successfully campaigned in the cabinet for the largest naval expenditure in British history.

Churchill adored Navy life aboard the Admiralty yacht, Enchantress, and after taking up office he set out to visit every capital ship and every Royal Navy base in the British Isles. He spent eight months of his first twelve in office aboard the yacht.

Churchill didn't just improve the Royal Navy. He reshaped it from the ground up. He brought in larger, more powerful ships and then modernized them by changing their fuel from coal to oil. His moves were instrumental and near prophetic in preparing the Royal Navy for the First World War.

Chapter 3: The First World War

By the time the First World War rolled around like the dark thundercloud that it was, Churchill had already closed the barn and shut the windows, so to speak. He had already launched a test mobilization of the navy and vehemently pushed the need to resist Germany. On August 2, 1914, he ordered the naval mobilization in order to ensure complete readiness upon the day when war was declared. Unlike the previous wars Churchill—and the rest of history—had seen, the First World War was an event of global catastrophe. Entire continents were to be painted in blood. This war would require all of Churchill's physical, psychological, and intellectual energy.

In typical Churchill fashion, when Antwerp was threatened in October 1914, he personally rushed to its defense. The battle was ultimately lost, but it came as a sort of victory for the Brits and Belgians, a sort of Pyrrhic victory for their enemies. While the public perceived Antwerp's fall as a disillusioning defeat, the Belgian Army was able to escape, and the Channel ports were saved. During Churchill's tenure in the Admiralty, his partnership with Admiral Sir John Fisher was characterized by dynamism as well as dissension. Within a year after its outbreak in August 1914, World War One had produced a bloody stalemate for the British and French on the Western Front and serious setbacks for the Russians on the Eastern Front. Allied military officials needed solutions, so they looked south. Invading the Gallipoli Peninsula via the Dardanelles Strait, reinforcing Russia, and knocking Turkey out of the war looked promising.

The aim of the campaign was to force the straits open to enable direct communication with Russia. The Admiralty war group and Asquith both supported de Robeck over Churchill when the naval attack failed and was immediately called off by Admiral J.M. de

Robeck. Churchill now faced political attack, which only intensified when Fisher resigned. Having been caught up with various departmental affairs, Churchill had had no time to prepare for the storm that broke out above and around him.

His involvement in the coalition government was nonexistent, and he was powerless when the Conservative party, with the exception of Sir William Maxwell Aitken (later Lord Beaverbrook), insisted that he be demoted from the Admiralty to the duchy of Lancaster. As a consolation, he was given special responsibility for the Gallipoli Campaign—a land as opposed to naval assault on the straits—but he did not have any actual powers of direction. Churchill faced a great many setbacks in his lifetime, but the failure of the attack on the Dardanelles during the Gallipoli Campaign proved one of the most devastating. While Churchill did not invent the Dardanelles strategy, he did endorse and ultimately champion it. Other ideas and strategies were debated, but in the end, Dardanelles seemed too perfect to fail so miserably. One reason behind this line of thinking was that the British were the naval superpower of the day, a second was that troops from Australia and New Zealand were not yet committed in France.

Though the Dardanelles Commission would later absolve Churchill of most of the blame for the military failure, he was to remain the most vocal champion of the strategic move to cut off the Turkish support of the Ottoman Empire in the First World War. When the plan failed, mostly due to a lack of military coordination between the army and navy, as well as hesitancy on the part of the commanders, Churchill was forced to reluctantly resign his ministerial post of First Lord of the Admiralty. Churchill later wrote:

> The campaign of the Dardanelles had been starved and crippled at every stage by the continued opposition of the

French and British High Commands in France to the withdrawal of troops and munitions from the main theatre of the war.

The Dardanelles failure was a crisis for the government, one that they could not take direct blame for. While Churchill had been a mere endorser of the strategy at first, he still took the blame, as he played one of the largest roles in its execution. In order to remain in the post of Prime Minister, Asquith had to form a coalition with the Conservatives. Churchill, the supposed mastermind of the disaster, was the price the Conservatives demanded, and in order to appease them, he was removed from the Admiralty and publicly blamed for the debacle. He did, however, remain in the cabinet by occupying a mostly ceremonial post until he himself resigned in November 1915.

Being the overachiever he was, this colossal failure was damaging to his reputation and ego. His resignation was a devastating personal and political blow to him. During this time, Churchill sunk into a great depression, which he referred to as a "black dog" that followed him around. After resigning, he decided to spend time volunteering to fight on the front in France. While he was waiting to be shipped off to France, he decided to take up painting as a hobby to help with his depression. He needed to do something, or else his depression would have gotten even worse. During his months in depressed states, his energy levels were low, and he would often do nothing but lay in bed until a burst of energy would resurrect him. He displayed symptoms of what would nowadays be referred to as bipolar disorder. So severe was this condition that his wife, Clementine, remarked, "I thought he would never get over the Dardanelles; I thought he would die of grief."

Today, his decision to take up painting as a counter to this depressed state is known as "art therapy." He started this practice at forty years old, allowing his creativity and inspiration to shine through in another aspect of his life. Painting soon became a passion, taking up much of his time and becoming an enjoyable lifelong hobby. He was even acknowledged by professionals, who thought that he had become quite the amateur painter, and that he could have been quite successful as a professional painter with further training. In 1948, he was appointed Honorary Academician Extraordinary by the Royal Academy for "achievements in the art of painting".

When in France

When he became a Liberal, he allied himself with a friend, mentor, and occasional enemy-in-arms David Lloyd George, who had initially encouraged him to change alliances. Lloyd George became Prime Minister of a wartime collation in 1916 and was instrumental in helping Churchill rehabilitate his political image after the disaster of the Gallipoli campaign the previous year. Churchill arrived in France in November 1916. If the assignment lived up to his expectations, he would have ranked as Brigade and Brigadier General, but Prime Minister Asquith vetoed any high command. Because of this, Churchill was given command of a battalion of the 6th Royal Scots Fusiliers with the rank of Lieutenant Colonel.

The battalion—not to mention most of the country—knew about Churchill's history as a failed politician. So, they viewed his role and rank with skepticism. But thanks to Churchill's personality, military experience, and knowledge, their reservations quickly faded.

One key quality that appealed to all was his cool-headed fearlessness. This allowed Churchill to lead by example, and as such, his men found it far easier to follow. He would frequently venture into No Man's Land, a strip of battlefield between trenches that could be anywhere from 50 yards to half a mile in width, during night patrol, despite the dangers it presented. One companion relayed:

> He never fell when a shell went off; he never ducked when a bullet went past with its loud crack. He used to say, after watching me duck: "It's no damn use ducking; the bullet has gone a long way past you by now."

Trench warfare is an iconic part of World War One. Most people today are familiar with it, some of the dangers it presented, and many have seen at least one Hollywood depiction of it. Trench warfare did not involve just one trench on either side, however. There were front-line trenches backed by support trenches. Trenches for reserve troops were farther back still. Communication trenches linked all trenches and were used to bring supplies and reinforcements forward.

Even though trenches were built for protection, they only provided protection from certain things to a certain degree. In other words, they were not necessarily places of safety. Artillery and gunfire caused around 33% of the casualties suffered in the trenches. The fire was so heavy that even today, over 100 years later, shell casings and ammo can still be found in the blood-soaked dirt. But many of the dangers lurked inside the trenches, not outside. As rats fed on corpses, they grew to the size of cats. The Trench Fever was carried by lice. There was a risk of gangrene and amputation due to the constant dampness that caused trench foot. If that wasn't enough, there was the smell—rotting flesh, stagnant water, overflowing latrines, unwashed bodies, gunpowder, cigarette smoke, and molding sandbags—the stench of death, claustrophobia, poor sanitation, and disease. Churchill's discipline was tough but fair, and he paid attention to how his men lived.

In light of all these horrid circumstances, Churchill's advice was ridiculously optimistic, but was received as brilliant by everyone everywhere:

> Don't be careless about yourselves - on the other hand not too careful. Keep a special pair of boots to sleep in & only get them muddy in a real emergency. Use alcohol in moderation but don't have a great parade of bottles in your dugouts. Live well but do not flaunt it. Laugh a little & teach your men to laugh - great good hum'r under fire - war is a game that is played with a smile. If you can't smile, grin. If you can't grin, keep out of the way till you can.

In France, as Churchill watched the consequences of governmental policies he had opposed, he grew frustrated. Churchill returned to Parliament as a private member six months after his casualty-depleted battalion was merged with another unit.

Fish Out of War

In October 1916, Asquith resigned as Prime Minister and was succeeded by Lloyd George. In May 1917, Lloyd George sent Churchill to inspect the front lines of the French War. Due to the long period of time that he had spent serving on the front lines in France after his resignation from government, Churchill was brought back into the government by Lloyd George as Minister of Munitions in 1917. It was a controversial decision, and though Churchill would again switch parties and would not always be politically aligned with Lloyd George, their lifelong friendship would endure.

The Conservatives were unwilling to consider his inclusion in the government until 1917, so he was not involved with the intrigues that led to the formation of a coalition government under Lloyd George. The Dardanelles commission report was published in March 1917, and it showed beyond a shadow of a doubt that Churchill was no more to blame for the fiasco than his colleagues; some even suggested that he was completely innocent, other than endorsing the idea.

Predictably, Churchill faced a strong reaction against the appointment, but this opposition came from more than just his opposers; it also came from members of Churchill's own party. The press attacked vociferously, and the pressure mounted when both the First Lord of the Admiralty and the Secretary for War threatened to resign.

Eventually, this opposition was overcome due to the simple fact that his opposers had bigger problems. Ultimately, Churchill's appointment was not a matter substantial enough to be allowed to threaten the wartime coalition.

His position as Minister of Munitions in July 1917 was a fairly new, but equally useful position to have. Though only two years old, the department employed over 2,500,000 men and women and was managed by a civil service that included well over 18,000.

It exercised greater control over what were generally regarded as the "privacies of life"—things like citizens, general assets, and the collective energies of the country—than any other arm of the British government. The First World War called for citizens to become soldiers, private assets to become national assets, and the collective energies of the country to be engaged in the struggle against the war. The Ministry of Munitions sought to do just that. The Ministry exercised most of its authority over Britain's working class and industrial resources. Once again, Churchill demonstrated his initiative and creativity by throwing himself into the office at full speed ahead.

First, among other things, he negotiated an end to a strike at factories that produced munitions along the Clyde faster than anyone else could have and single-handedly increased munitions production. Later, in June 1918, he brought a second strike to its knees by threatening to conscript those engaged in the strike into the army. That same year, Churchill voted in support of the Representation of the People Act 1918 in the House of Commons, an act that gave some British women the right to vote. Then, in November 1918, four days after the Armistice, Churchill's fourth child, Marigold, was born.

Excluded from the cabinet, Churchill played a largely administrative role. However, the effort he had thrown into developing and producing the tank, a project he had initiated at the Admiralty, greatly sped up the use of the weapon that was to break through the deadlock on the Western Front. Churchill promised that he would stick to making weapons, not plans, but he nonetheless involved himself with all matters of strategy and tactics for the remainder of World War One.

Ironically, Churchill was only returned to a service department after the war ended, meaning his full utility was never seen during the First World War. In 1919, after the war was over and munitions production was halted, Lloyd George appointed Churchill to the War Office. In spite of Winston wanting vengeance for his earlier dismissal from the admiralty, he accepted when he was offered to be both Secretary of State for War and the Secretary of State for Air simultaneously.

In this role, Churchill faced two pressing issues. First, he had to manage the demobilization of nearly three million soldiers. Second was the issue of British troops, who were initially sent to Russia to support the war against Germany and restore the Czarist government and were now caught in the middle of Russia's civil war. To best manage the issue of demobilization, Churchill established a system that released soldiers based on length of time in service, their wounds, and family circumstances, a policy widely viewed as fair and effective. Dealing with the British troops in Russia was another matter. Although the British government initially supported the Anti-Bolshevik (White) army, their policy regarding intervention in the Russian Civil War was inconsistent after the Revolutions of 1917 and the separate peace with Germany in 1918.

Churchill was a famous anti-Bolshevik, saying that "of all the tyrannies in history, the Bolshevik tyranny is the worst, the most destructive, the most degrading." That's not even to mention the famous line "Kill the Bolshie, kiss the Hun." However, Churchill argued both sides of the issue and produced a mountain of memos while trying to convince his government to adopt a policy—any policy. Churchill's enemies took this as an opportunity to characterize him as "unreliable" and "unsteady." In their eyes, he was at best, a vacillator, and at worse, a warmonger.

Churchill zealously presided over cutting military expenditures, and for most of his tenure in the War Office, Churchill was preoccupied with the Allied intervention in Russia. Churchill, being the passionately anti-Bolshevik Brit that he was, secured from the cabinet an intensification and prolongation of British involvement in Russia, despite the divided and loosely organized state that the cabinet was in at the time. This policy was far beyond the wishes of Parliament or the nation. Afterward, in 1920, after the last British forces had been withdrawn, Churchill wound up playing a major role in having arms sent to the Poles when they moved to invade Ukraine.

In 1918, while acting as Assistant Secretary of the US Navy, Franklin Roosevelt made a visit to Great Britain. He was welcomed to the country in Portsmouth and was then driven to London, where he was placed under protection at the Ritz Hotel in Piccadilly.

While in the country, Roosevelt toured the British and American bases at the invitation of the First Lord of the Admiralty, Sir Eric Geddes. During the tour, he met with a number of officials, including Prime Minister David Lloyd George and Foreign Secretary Arthur Balfour. He was later granted a forty-five-minute-long audience with King George VI, which was probably the highlight of his visit. During his first official trip to Great Britain, Roosevelt attended a dinner at Gray's Inn in London, and it was here that he first met Winston Churchill. But contrary to what one may assume about the meeting based on the character of these two individuals, neither seemed impressed with the other at first. In fact, Roosevelt seemed to be downright unimpressed.

Roosevelt later said that "I always disliked him since the time I went to England in 1917 or 1918. At a dinner I attended he acted like a stinker." To make matters worse, Churchill later failed to recall this first meeting. Despite this unpleasant first encounter, they later became great friends and confidants during the Second World War. Like many of history's great minds, they were drawn to each other, if not repelled at first.

Chapter 4: After the War

After the war, Lloyd George called a general election. The vote would occur on December 14, 1918, and Churchill was to be a part of it. He called for the creation of the League of Nations in order to try and prevent future wars, as well as to make smaller changes, such as the nationalization of railways and tax reform. While the Conservatives won, Lloyd George maintained his position as Prime Minister and appointed Churchill to serve as both post-war Secretary of State for War and Secretary of State for Air in the War Office from January 1919 until he became Colonial Secretary in February 1921. While in the War Office, he was responsible for the demobilization of the British army, as well as the maintenance of one million conscripted men for the British Army of the Rhine.

The British Empire reached its peak due to the amount of territory that had been brought under its control after the end of World War One. However, Britain was still battered and bruised after the war—low on resources and the men needed to replenish them. The burden of enforcing its newly expanded empire further sapped Britain of what little it had left.

In international affairs, Churchill stood in opposition to the demeaning measures levied against the now-defeated Germany, which proved to be the wiser outlook, seeing as how Germany returned as the main villain in the Second World War. He even opposed the notion that the German army should be demobilized, suggesting that they could be used as a sort of bulwark against Soviet Russia. While he was anti-communist, he did not extend British support to the Whites (a confederation of anti-Bolsheviks and anti-Communists) in Russia for too long, as he recognized the need for the British soldiers to return home after a long-fought war.

Rise and Fall of a Secretary

The year 1921 was one that could truly be described as being full of blood, sweat, and tears, highs and lows, advances, and tragedy. Churchill took up the position of Secretary of State for the Colonies in February 1921. This was certainly a major victory. February 1921 to October 1921 saw the bulk of his work done in this position negotiating the Anglo-Irish Treaty, which ended up being signed in December 1921. The remainder of his time was spent implementing the conditions of the treaty, as well as conducting relations with the newborn Irish Free State.

Earlier in the year, in March 1921, the first exhibit featuring Churchill's paintings was held in Paris. This must have been a memorable occasion for Churchill, as painting had become a favored passion of his. Even though he exhibited under a pseudonym, it was obvious that the paintings were not created by normal talents. Following this high point, however, just two months later, in May 1921, Churchill's mother passed away. This was a horrible loss, but it was to pale in comparison to what happened next.

In August 1921, Churchill's dear daughter, Marigold, the youngest in the family at the time, passed away at just over 2 years old. She had contracted septicemia while on holiday with the children's governess earlier in the year. Her affectionate nickname, "Duckadilly," was never to be used again. The loss was a harsh blow to both Winston and Clementine, one that neither recovered from for the remainder of their days.

But the work was far from done, and being the man he was, Churchill didn't let his pain or sadness prevent him from progressing. While in the Colonial Office, his time was also spent taking care of the mandated territories in the Middle East. Churchill's policies were as follows:

> For the costly British forces in the area, he substituted a reliance on the air force and the establishment of rulers congenial to British interests; for this settlement of Arab affairs, he relied heavily on the advice of T.E. Lawrence. For Palestine, where he inherited conflicting pledges to Jews and Arabs, he produced in 1922 the White Paper that confirmed Palestine as a Jewish national home while recognizing continuing Arab rights. Churchill never had departmental responsibility for Ireland, but he progressed from an initial belief in firm, even ruthless, maintenance of British rule to an active role in the negotiations that led to the Irish treaty of 1921. Subsequently, he gave full support to the new Irish government.

Though it had already been a tumultuous year, it would only continue to go downhill from there. In the fall of 1922, Churchill developed appendicitis, and had to be taken to the hospital, where he was operated on. While recovering from the operation in the hospital in October 1922, he lost something else. This wasn't a literal piece of himself, but it was a figurative piece of himself.

Lloyd George's Liberal Party coalition was dissolved, and in the General Election of 1922, Churchill lost his Dundee seat to a man named Edwin Scrymgeour. He did not go down without a fight.

While Churchill was in the hospital, his wife, Clementine, and their 7-week-old daughter, Mary, went out to represent him in his constituency. The press not only insulted Winston and Clementine, but they even stooped as low as to call poor Mary the Churchill's "unbaptised infant". It would seem that some things—especially the press—never change.

Clementine fought well and hard, speaking at six meetings before vociferous and volatile crowds, one of which was broken up by an attack with sneezing powder. After recovering, he too went and spoke at Caird Hall to the friendlier crowds, and then to Drill Hall, where the usual angry mob awaited him. He wrote that "I was struck by the looks of passionate hatred on the faces of some of the younger men and women. Indeed, but for my helpless condition, I am sure they would have attacked me."

He was out of Parliament in 1922 and 1923, losing By-elections each year.

He later wrote that during this time he was "without an office, without a seat, without a party, and without an appendix."

Back to Writing

Churchill spent the next two years, from 1922-1924, in a sort of limbo state, having been exiled from parliament with no way of getting back with the Liberals, and still having his name leave a bad taste in the mouth of the Conservatives. However, it was the Conservative party that would turn out to be his redemption.

For the six months following the loss of the Dundee seat, Churchill spent a lot of his time at the Villa Rêve d'Or near Cannes, where he threw himself into his creative endeavors, namely painting and writing.

His autobiographical account of the First World War, *The World Crisis*, was written during this time, and the first volume was published the following year, in April 1923. It was the first of many, and the rest were to be written and published over the following ten years.

After the six months were up, he returned to politics with renewed gusto. He first tried with the Liberals again. In 1923, after the calling of the general election, he was asked by seven Liberal associates to stand as their candidate. Out of the seven, he ended up settling for Leicester West, a constituency that was represented in the House of Commons in the United Kingdom's Parliament. However, he did not win the seat.

Andrew Bonar Law, the leader of the Conservative party, took Lloyd George and the Liberal's place as Prime Minister. But the battle was not over. Later on, in March 1924, he stood as an independent anti-socialist candidate. He was alienated from the support of the Liberals, and he hadn't yet gained much favor with the Conservatives.

He was defeated once again, but he pushed on to the next opportunity. In May 1924, he gave a radical speech at Liverpool. Having seen the effect that socialism and communism had had on the world, he strongly advocated against them, going as far as to say that the Liberal party had no place in politics and that they should support the Conservatives if they were to stop the Labour Party and truly eradicate the socialists.

In Churchill's view, only the Conservative Party had a strong enough base to successfully defeat Socialism. He therefore felt that it was the responsibility of the Liberals to join forces with the Conservatives on a broad progressive platform. In a conversation between Baldwin and Churchill, Baldwin asked "Are you willing to help us?" to which Churchill replied, "Yes, if you really want me." Churchill would later recount his acceptance of the post of Chancellor. What he had wanted to reply was "Will the bloody duck swim?" but, as he later wrote, "as it was a formal and important conversation I replied, 'This fulfils my ambition. I still have my father's robe as Chancellor. I shall be proud to serve you in this splendid Office.'"

Churchill then returned to Chartwell. There, he later recalled, "I had the greatest difficulty in convincing my wife that I was not merely teasing her." Churchill's friends were equally thrilled. Former chairman of the Parliamentary Liberal Party, George Lambert, wrote: "Winston dear boy, I have got a fair instinct for politics. I think I shall live to see you Prime Minister."

Churchill's appointment as Chancellor led to him finally regaining a seat in the General Election of 1924. After Winston negotiated a return to the Conservative Party, he managed to become Chancellor of the Exchequer, a position that had also been held by his father. After becoming Chancellor as a Conservative on November 6, 1924, he intended to pursue his free-trade principles by uplifting laissez-faire economics. However, after the defeat of the Conservatives on May 30, 1929, Churchill was out of power again. To add insult to injury, the Wall Street Crash of 1929 followed his political loss and left him without a penny to his name. Once again, he took up pen and paper, beginning a period of writing to regain both his political notoriety and economic status.

Chapter 5: The Prophecy Comes True

After 1929, Churchill spent ten years bouncing between positions and gaining new life experiences. At first, when out of political power, his "black dog" threatened to come bounding back to him. He turned to writing for solace and composed *Marlborough: His Life and Times*, a four-volume long biography of his ancestor, John Churchill, 1st Duke of Marlborough, to distract himself from the depression that kept trying to return. It was during this period that he indulged heavily in alcohol, though some claim the extent of his alcoholism is greatly exaggerated.

He tried to establish a Conservative-Liberal coalition, which gained him Baldwin's further favor, published his autobiography, *My Early Life*, and in 1931, resigned from his position in the Conservative Shadow Cabinet because Baldwin supported the Labour government's decision to grant Dominion status to India. He even opposed Mohandas Gandhi, better known as Mahatma Gandhi. Later on, in October 1931, the Conservatives won by a large margin and Churchill near doubled his majority in Epping. Despite this, he was granted no ministerial position.

In January 1932, he returned to America to give more lectures. He finished them all by March and returned home. Later that same year, he decided to visit his ancestor's battlefields in a place that he may have guessed would be his own in the near future. These past and future battlefields were in Germany.

He stayed in Munich, and in a stunning event of foreshadowing, he met Hitler's good friend, Ernst Hanfstaengl, a man who was also rising in prominence. Hanfstaengl even attempted to arrange a meeting between Churchill and Hitler, but the dictator was unimpressed and didn't oblige. Churchill told Hanfstaengl

"Tell your boss from me that anti-Semitism may be a good starter, but it is a bad sticker."

The next time they came close to meeting was in the middle of the greatest bloodbath in the history of mankind. The time leading up to that bloodbath was ticking away, but there was still so much left to be done.

First Lord of the Admiralty

Churchill was appointed as First Lord of the Admiralty on September 3, 1939. That same day, the British declared war on Germany following the outbreak of World War Two. This was the same position he had held during the First World War, only this time, he expounded upon it in a brilliant display of competence that led up to his final goal.

He was a member of Prime Minister Chamberlain's war cabinet, which Chamberlain himself led against the Germans for the first eight months of the war.

This time period was also marked by what was known as the "Phony War," during which the only significant action taken by British forces was at sea. When they returned on December 13, 1939, Churchill congratulated them on a "brilliant sea fight," and said that their actions in a "cold, dark winter had warmed the cockles of the British heart."

Later on, in February 1940, Churchill learned about prisoners who were being held aboard a German supply ship, and ordered the captain of the destroyer *HMS Cossack*, Phillip Vian, to board the ship in Norwegian waters and liberate them. There were 300 prisoners liberated that day, and combined with his speeches, personality, and ambition, Churchill's name only grew bigger and garnered more attention.

The German activity in the Baltic Sea made Churchill nervous, and he had initially wanted to send a naval force to dampen the situation and keep the Germans at bay. But there was a change of plans that involved this relatively minor defensive move becoming a full-blown operation of its own. They called it *Operation Wilfred*. It went as follows:

> The operation had been mooted as a means of preventing German coastal ships from sailing to the south in Norwegian territorial waters with high-grade iron ore. The iron ore was shifted by rail from the Luleå region of Sweden, whose Baltic coast was ice-bound in the winter months, to the Norwegian port of Narvik, which was ice-free even in the winter. The Allies wished to prevent the iron traffic to Germany as a high priority, but felt that the implementation of "Wilfred" might force the Norwegians into the German camp or require the landing of Allied ground forces in Norway to prevent the Norwegians from sweeping the minefields. The British finally decided to implement 'Wilfred' on 7/8 April, with three fully publicized minefields to be laid in Norwegian waters and with ground forces prepared for rapid delivery to Norway should the situation demand it.

The plan to prevent Germans from occupying Norway ultimately failed. However, it set off a chain reaction that ended with Churchill's long-awaited rise to the top. After the failure, the Commons held an open debate that lasted two days, from May 7-9, 1940, to discuss how the government was handling the war.

This debate is now referred to as the Norway Debate and is widely regarded as one of the most significant events in parliament history. On May 8, 1940, the second day of the debate, the Labour opposition called for a decision that essentially led to a vote of no confidence (also called "a motion of no confidence") in Chamberlain's government.

In the end, the government won the vote, but the majority who voted in favor of it had been greatly reduced over the two days of debating. In the end, the forming of a coalition that Chamberlain needed was denied by Labour, who said that they would only accept a different Conservative. The only two men for the job were Churchill and Lord Halifax. At long last, Churchill was to assume the post he had aspired to. Churchill was to be Prime Minister.

Churchill, Prime Minister

Churchill was 65 years old when he became Prime Minister. But he had the same spark of fearless aggression that he had when he was 20. The stars seemed to align for this position; he had no chance of winning it through a general election, and he had been unpopular with the Conservatives at the time of his selection. Though Chamberlain had remained Prime Minister for a short time, cancer forced him to resign sooner, and he died that November.

Churchill started his leadership by forming a 5-man war cabinet. The cabinet grew and changed as the year went on and ended up with 8 members. This was a new war cabinet that was oriented towards winning, unlike Chamberlain's.

Churchill also took up the position of Minister of Defence, which made him the most powerful wartime Prime Minister in the history of Britain. He was wise enough to select people he knew and trusted to take part in government. Men and women who, when combined and working towards the same goal, would be able to bring down the enemy war machines of Germany and the Axis powers. He didn't discriminate politically. If he thought a person fit the role, he picked them, regardless of their party affiliation. His government included those on the far right, like Lord Lloyd, and those on the far left, like Ellen Wilkinson.

Chapter 6: Waging the Second World War

By the end of May 1940, hope for a British victory seemed to be dwindling. Even Churchill himself seemed to be developing a negative outlook on the situation. The British Expeditionary Force was in retreat to Dunkirk, and the fall of France seemed inevitable. Halifax, one of the war cabinet members, proposed that the government try to take a peaceful route out.

Churchill wanted to fight, even if France fell into enemy hands. He saw that to take a peaceful way out would be no better, if not worse, than fighting it out to the bitter end. Even though he himself was worried about their chances of winning, he refused to surrender.

However, his view combined with the inspiring, nation-riling speeches he delivered managed to lift the weary British people out of the mud and to their feet. It was war, and there was to be no survival without victory.

Blitz and Pearls

Operation Dynamo, the operation that evacuated 338,226 allied servicemen from Dunkirk, ended on June 4, 1940. The number was staggeringly high and is still regarded as a miracle.

After the Battle of Britain, which was fought by the Royal Air Force (RAF), or, as Churchill referred to them after their victory, "The Few," the *Luftwaffe,* Germany's air force, decided to play dirty, and switched up their strategy to bomb London. This is now known as the "Blitz".

The Blitz grew even more intense during October and November, and the horrors that it brought lasted for a further eight months, when Hitler initiated Operation Barbarossa. Its purpose? Invade the Soviet Union. The purpose of the *Luftwaffe* was to reduce the production of British war assets as a precursor to the invasion. Unfortunately for them, the production only increased.

All other tasks and problems were overshadowed by Hitler's attack on the Soviet Union on June 22, 1941. It was not surprising, though. On April 3 of that year, Churchill had sent a personally drafted message for Stafford Cripps, a British ambassador in Moscow, for delivery to Joseph Stalin. However, there was something strange about it. While Churchill was normally blunt and forthright, his message to Stalin started by saying "I have sure information from a trusted agent."

The reason for Churchill's evasive manner was because the agent in question was no human being; it was a Bletchley decrypt, which was information he was not willing to reveal to Stalin.

Thus, when Churchill awoke one midsummer Sunday morning to the news of the German slaughter in Russia, he was not surprised. He had warned Stalin weeks prior. Despite his stature as the anti-communist, he had remarked that "If Hitler invaded Hell, I would at least make a favorable reference to the Devil." He knew what a threat the Germans were, and he was ready to stop them, even if it meant defending the Soviets.

Shortly thereafter, on December 7-8, 1941, the Japanese initiated dual offensive moves that led to Churchill's declaration of war on them. First, they attacked Pearl Harbor while America was still a neutral country, and then they invaded Malaya. Churchill knew that winning the war without America's participation would be exceedingly difficult, so he jumped at the opportunity to draw them in and declare war on Japan.

Soon after, Germany and Italy declared war on America. It was now an international conflict of a scale never seen before.

Churchill went to Washington that same month to meet with President Franklin D. Roosevelt for the Washington Conference, where the decision was made that a European victory was more important than one in the Pacific. Roosevelt agreed that Hitler was the enemy, and that defeating him would be the most imperative step toward Allied victory.

D-Day

D-Day was being planned for almost a year before it happened. On May 19, 1943, Prime Minister Churchill and President Roosevelt set a date for the cross-Channel landing that would become D-Day. They decided on May 1, 1944, which proved to be premature, as bad weather would be a factor. In front of a joint session of Congress, Churchill warned against the "dragging-out of the war at enormous expense." He was concerned that the Allies would become "tired or bored or split" and play into the hands of Germany and Japan. So, he pushed for an early and massive attack on the "underbelly of the Axis." In an effort to speed things up, Churchill and Roosevelt planned the cross-Channel invasion of Normandy, in northern France, for May 1, 1944. They chose to ignore the potential problems presented by the invasion of Italy, which would then be underway. It would be carried out by 29 divisions, potentially even including a Free

French division. Despite their careful planning, the D-Day invasion did not take place until June 6, 1944.

Churchill anticipated a death count of around 20,000 men. However, D-Day was marked by 8,000 dead. Churchill visited Normandy for the first time only six days later, on June 12. He went to the Montgomery HQ, which was about 5 miles inland, and that same evening, while on his way back to London, the first flying bombs were launched. In the months that followed, from September 1944 to February 1945, Churchill, Roosevelt, and Foreign Secretary of the Churchill War Cabinet, Anthony Eden attended three conferences: the Quebec Conference, the Moscow Conference, and the Yalta Conference.

Approximately 1,200 British and American bombers attacked Dresden between February 13-15, 1945, during which time the wounded and refugees from the Eastern Front were crammed into the city. Churchill had launched the campaign in January in an effort to shorten the war by bombing specific areas. As the war wound down, Churchill regretted the bombing because it appeared to have resulted in excessive civilian casualties. In 2010, an independent commission confirmed a death toll between 22,700 and 25,000. In a memorandum written to General Ismay for the Chiefs of Staff Committee on March 28, 1945, Churchill decided to restrict area bombing: "The destruction of Dresden remains a serious query against the conduct of Allied bombing... I feel the need for more precise concentration upon military objectives... rather than on mere acts of terror and wanton destruction, however impressive."

According to British historian Frederick Taylor, Allied bombings killed roughly the same number of German citizens as Soviet bombings killed Soviet citizens. Jenkins posits that Churchill was moved more by dread than regret. According to him, President Truman's use of the second atomic bomb on Nagasaki six months later was no more reprehensible than the area bombing campaign.

Several weeks later, on May 7, 1945, at the SHAEF headquarters in Reims, the Allies accepted Germany's surrender. Churchill's broadcast to the nation on Victory in Europe Day announced that Germany had surrendered and that a final ceasefire would go into effect on all fronts in Europe at midnight that night, May 8, 1945. In the aftermath of this announcement, Churchill joined the Royal Family on the balcony at Buckingham Palace, where he appeared before a large crowd of citizens. From the palace, he went to Whitehall, where he told the next large crowd "God bless you all. This is your victory. In our long history, we have never seen a greater day than this. Everyone, man or woman, has done their best." That evening, Churchill made another broadcast to the nation, assuring the country that Japan would be defeated in the coming months. Japan surrendered on August 15, 1945.

Churchill resigned as prime minister on May 23, 1945, due to the first general election in almost a decade, along with the Labour ministers' refusal to continue the wartime coalition. As part of the National Government, which was similar to the Conservative-dominated coalition of the 1930s, he formally accepted the invitation to form the Churchill Caretaker Ministry. Since overseas votes needed to be collected for the 1945 elections, results were not known until July 26, despite the fact that voting day was July 5. After a landslide victory by Labour, Churchill stepped down as prime minister and was succeeded by Clement Attlee. Despite being unopposed by the major parties in Woodford, his new constituency in Essex, Churchill won over a single independent by a much smaller margin than expected. After hearing the results from Woodford, he anticipated national defeat by Labour and, when Clementine said that it might be "a blessing in disguise," he retorted that "at the moment it seems very effectively disguised."

Thus, 1945 marked the year that ended Churchill's 5-year stretch as Prime Minister. He was arguably the most important Allied leader in the Second World War and is still regarded as one of the most brilliant war strategists to have ever lived.

Conclusion

Churchill is remembered for a good reason. Many sources used to write this book were taken from organizations and societies that were formed just a few years after his death. Even now, there are conventions held about his life and accomplishments, museums dedicated to him, and books written about him.

A man that celebrated must have been worth remembering, and there is still much to learn from the legacy he left behind.

While his career had many ups and downs, both politically and personally, it was one that ended with the fulfillment of what he had sensed for the longest time: the calling of greatness. Even today, he is still one of the most well-known Prime Ministers worldwide.

While he had luck on his side, he also dedicated himself to the course of life that he deemed to be the most worthwhile, and in the end, lived long enough to reap the rewards.

Churchill suffered a major heart attack in 1953 while still in office, and in January 1965, he passed away at the age of 90. Churchill's obituary, broadcasted by the BBC, tells the story of a great man, and shares further insight into his life:

> "Winston Churchill is dead." The words are like great boulders falling silently down a cliff into the sea. For those who are old enough to remember one (or both) of the World Wars, there can be no doubt whatsoever; the greatest man of our age has gone from among us. Of all the tributes paid to him during his lifetime and since his going I choose the one made at the time of his retirement as Prime Minister: "Not only did he shape and write history: He is History itself." I had the privilege of hearing

Sir Winston's last major speech in the House of Commons on March the First 1955 – just over a month before his retirement as Prime Minister. It was a survey of the sombre world situation. Sir Winston paused, placed his hands around the despatch box (about the size of a small suitcase), lying on the Commons table and said, "It is now the fact that a quantity of plutonium, probably less than would fill this box on the table, would suffice to produce weapons which would give indisputable world domination to any great power which was the only one to have it." And it struck me how amazing it was that this very man, Prime Minister well into the second half of the twentieth century, had, as a young subaltern, taken part in the last great cavalry charge of the British Army at Omdurman in the Sudan in 1898. In the years between, he was the only statesman to play a major role in both world wars and incidentally to write the history of both in no less than ten volumes. His continuous membership of the House of Commons dated from 1924 – and, before, he had already sat for 21 years in Parliament, so that his membership spanned some 60 years. In that time, he held most of the great offices of State, including the 7 great years as Prime Minister. He began a Conservative; then crossed the floor of the House and served for 16 years with the Liberals taking (it is often forgotten) a leading part in the introduction of major social reforms before the first world war. Back with the Conservatives again after 1922 he was one of their sharpest critics in the years before the second world war. He won his greatest fame as the Leader of the all-party war time coalition. Then rebuffed by the electorate in 1945 he busied himself with the causes close to his heart, including the unification of Europe- and returned to No. 10 Downing Street in 1951, to retire four years later, in his eightieth year. Yet he found the time to write more than 30 volumes (for which he was awarded the Nobel Prize for literature, to compose thousands of speeches, some of which will endure forever in the anthologies of great oratory, to travel throughout the world, first as a war correspondent, then as a statesman. And just to "fill in time" he painted with very considerable ability – and, when he was younger, was an enthusiastic amateur brick-layer. The world will not see his like again.

And the world has not seen his likes, before or since. Churchill is singular amongst the annals of history, and his life and legacy are not one that will be soon forgotten.

References

America's National Churchill Museum. (n.d.-a). *America's national churchill museum | glow worm, winston churchill leadership.* Www.nationalchurchillmuseum.org. https://www.nationalchurchillmuseum.org/winston-churchill-leadership-the-glow-worm.html

America's National Churchill Museum. (n.d.-b). *National churchill museum | winston churchill in world war I and its aftermath.* Www.nationalchurchillmuseum.org. https://www.nationalchurchillmuseum.org/churchill-in-world-war-i-and-aftermath.html

America's National Churchill Museum. (1969). *America's national churchill museum | winston churchill interwar period.* Www.nationalchurchillmuseum.org. https://www.nationalchurchillmuseum.org/sir-winston-churchill-interwar-period.html

Belfast News-Letter, & Creative Centenaries. (1921, February 14). *Winston churchill appointed secretary of state for the colonies*. Creative Centenaries.

https://www.creativecentenaries.org/on-this-
day/winston-churchill-appointed-secretary-of-state-for-
the-colonies

Codenames, & Chant, C. (2020). *Wilfred | operations &
codenames of WWII*. Codenames.info.

https://codenames.info/operation/wilfred/

Cooper, M. (1981). *The german air force 1933-1945 : An
anatomy of failure*. Jane's.

Encyclopædia Britannica, inc. (n.d.). *Leadership during World
War II*. Encyclopædia Britannica.

https://www.britannica.com/biography/Winston-
Churchill/Leadership-during-World-War-II

Gilbert, M. (1991). *Churchill: A life*. Heinemann.

Hansard, & House of Commons. (1940). *War situation*.

Api.parliament.uk. https://api.parliament.uk/historic-
hansard/commons/1940/aug/20/war-
situation#column_1167

Hermiston, R. (2017). *All behind you, winston : Churchill's
great coalition 1940-45*. Aurum Press.

History.com Editors. (2009, November 5). *FDR and Winston Churchill plot d-day*. HISTORY; A&E Television Networks. https://www.history.com/this-day-in-history/churchill-and-fdr-plot-d-day#:~:text=On%20May%2019%2C%201943%2C%20British

International Churchill Society. (1905, December 1). *Named under-secretary of state for the colonies*. International Churchill Society. https://winstonchurchill.org/the-life-of-churchill/rising-politician/named-under-secretary-of-state-for-the-colonies/

International Churchill Society. (1911, October 25). *Churchill appointed first lord of the admiralty*. International Churchill Society. https://winstonchurchill.org/the-life-of-churchill/rising-politician/churchill-appointed-first-lord-of-the-admiralty/

International Churchill Society. (1915, July 2). *Begins oil painting at hoe farm, surrey*. International Churchill Society. https://winstonchurchill.org/the-life-of-churchill/rising-politician/begins-oil-painting-at-hoe-farm-surrey-2/

International Churchill Society. (1970, January 1). *Churchill proclaims he will "... save the empire."* International Churchill Society. https://winstonchurchill.org/the-life-of-churchill/child/churchill-proclaims-he-will-save-the-empire/

International Churchill Society. (2008a, June 18). *Orders, decorations and medals - the international churchill society*. The International Churchill Society; Churchill. https://winstonchurchill.org/the-life-of-churchill/young-soldier/orders-decorations-and-medals/

International Churchill Society. (2008b, October 14). *Churchill's elections*. International Churchill Society. https://winstonchurchill.org/resources/reference/churchills-elections/

International Churchill Society. (2008c, October 17). *London to ladysmith via pretoria*. International Churchill Society. https://winstonchurchill.org/the-life-of-churchill/young-soldier/london-to-ladysmith-via-

pretoria/

International Churchill Society. (2009a, February 12). *Lt.

churchill: 4th queen's own hussars.* International

Churchill Society. https://winstonchurchill.org/the-life-

of-churchill/young-soldier/lt-churchill-4th-queens-own-

hussars/

International Churchill Society. (2009b, February 13). *Harrow

school.* International Churchill Society.

https://winstonchurchill.org/the-life-of-

churchill/child/1886-1890/harrow-school/

International Churchill Society. (2015a, February 5). *Autumn

1900 (age 26).* International Churchill Society.

https://winstonchurchill.org/the-life-of-

churchill/young-soldier/1896-1900/autumn-1900-age-

26/

International Churchill Society. (2015b, March 12). *Autumn

1922 (age 48).* International Churchill Society.

https://winstonchurchill.org/the-life-of-churchill/rising-politician/1920-1932/autumn-1922-age-48/

International Churchill Society. (2017a). *Child archives - the international churchill society*. The International Churchill Society; Churchill. https://winstonchurchill.org/the-life-of-churchill/child/

International Churchill Society. (2017b). *The life of churchill archives - the international churchill society*. The International Churchill Society; Churchill. https://winstonchurchill.org/the-life-of-churchill/life/

Jenkins, R. (2002). *Churchill*. Pan Books.

Marr, A. (2010). *The making of modern Britain*. Pan Macmillan.

Nicholas, H. G., & Encyclopaedia Britannica. (2018). *Winston churchill | biography, world war II, & facts*. Encyclopædia Britannica. https://www.britannica.com/biography/Winston-Churchill

Olsen, J. D. (2021a, August 10). *Churchill appointed first lord of the admiralty*. International Churchill Society.

https://winstonchurchill.org/the-life-of-
churchill/rising-politician/churchill-appointed-first-
lord-of-the-admiralty/

Olsen, J. D., & International Churchill Society. (2021b, August
10). *Churchill gives his maiden speech in the house.*
International Churchill Society.
https://winstonchurchill.org/the-life-of-
churchill/rising-politician/churchill-gives-his-maiden-
speech-in-the-house/

Pixelstorm. (2021a, August 10). *Churchill proclaims he will '...
save the empire'.* International Churchill Society.
https://winstonchurchill.org/the-life-of-
churchill/child/churchill-proclaims-he-will-save-the-
empire/

Pixelstorm. (2021b, May 11). *The child.* International Churchill
Society. https://winstonchurchill.org/churchill-
central/storyline/the-child-2/

Pixelstorm. (2021c, May 11). *"The creeds of the devil": Churchill
between the two totalitarianisms, 1917-1945 (1 of 3).*
International Churchill Society.

https://winstonchurchill.org/publications/finest-hour-extras/the-creeds-of-the-devil-churchill-between-the-two-totalitarianisms-1917-1945-1-of-3/

Pixelstorm. (2021d, May 11). *Lt. Churchill: 4th Queen's Own Hussars.* International Churchill Society. https://winstonchurchill.org/the-life-of-churchill/young-soldier/lt-churchill-4th-queens-own-hussars/

P. T. C. (n.d.). *RAF Chapel.* Westminster Abbey. Retrieved August 6, 2022, from https://www.westminster-abbey.org/about-the-abbey/history/raf-chapel

Schneer, J. (2015). *Ministers at war : Winston churchill and his war cabinet.* Oneworld.

Spartacus Educational. (2017, December 17). *1923 general election.* Spartacus Educational. https://spartacus-educational.com/GE1923.htm

Taylor, F. (2004). *Dresden, tuesday, february 13, 1945.* Bloomsbury.

The National Archives. (2020, November 27). *Death of Winston Churchill.* The National Archives.

https://www.nationalarchives.gov.uk/education/resourc

es/sixties-britain/death-winston-churchill-2/

Virginia Tech. (n.d.). *History repeating*. Liberalarts.vt.edu.

https://liberalarts.vt.edu/magazine/2017/history-

repeating.html

Westminster Abbey. (n.d.). *RAF chapel*. Westminster Abbey.

https://www.westminster-abbey.org/about-the-

abbey/history/raf-chapel